# *Seven Levers for Success in Selling Real Estate*

Leverage Secrets from Top-Producing Agents

by Derek Tye

*Seven Levers for Success in Selling Real Estate*
© 2020 by Derek Tye
**www.KingdomRealEstateAgents.com**

This title is also available in Kindle format.

*All rights reserved. No part of this publication may be reproduced, stored in a retrieval system, or transmitted in any form or by any means--for example, electronic, photocopy, recording--without the prior written permission of the publisher.*

ISBN: 9798621126537

Printed in the United States of America

"When I first met Derek, I knew he not only had a great real estate business, he also had a heart to help others build a big business in real estate too. And, because our lives are autobiographical, it was no surprise to learn Derek is a great husband and father who has a tremendous love for God and is not afraid to show it. This is something the business world could use more of. I am positive the lessons Derek shares in this book will help you on your journey to build a business worth owning, a career worth having and a legacy worth leaving. Blessings!"
— *Linda McKissack, Author of 'Hold' and 'Presentation Mastery,' Owner of Keller Williams (KW) Ohio Valley Region, Seventh Level Realtor® and Millionaire Real Estate Investor*

"Derek has nailed it! I love the simplicity of this book. We all overcomplicate process of selling real estate, then can't understand why we are not successful. The main reason we (as a society) do not succeed like we should is that we want immediate gratification for everything we do. Doing what is right every day and delaying gratification is what leads to real, long-term success. That is what building a big business is all about. As Derek explains, stick to a plan and be consistent in your lead generation daily, follow up with those leads over time, wake up the next day, and do it all over again. Keep it simple to succeed!"
— *Myra Oliver, Millionaire Real Estate Investor, Real Estate Franchise Owner and Author of 'Down Home Money: A Simple Approach to Financial Freedom'*

"Derek's *Seven Levers for Success in Selling Real Estate* is a must-have practical guide on how to build a big real estate business the right way. Whether you are a new agent or a seasoned

agent hitting your growth ceiling, this book walks you through what you should be focusing on, while leaving out the fluff that simply doesn't matter. By reading and executing his seven levers, you'll naturally reach the success you deserve, while also living a life by design."
— *Ricky Cain, Realtor® in Austin, Texas*

"I met Derek about five years ago when I was invited to teach to a group of agents and investors who were embarking on the journey of opening a new Keller Williams Realty franchise. I was immediately impressed with his clarity and authenticity around real estate, business, God and family. He really impressed me as an entrepreneurial leader and businessman. I presented that day and shared a little about my journey in the 30+ years in new construction sales, real estate sales and leadership experience. Derek and I connected later that day and I have enjoyed watching his journey and truly call him a friend. This book applies the KISS principles to the path of a successful real estate career, as Derek's shares his stories along the way."
— *Sue Parrish, Operating Principal, Investor in four KW offices and Realtor®, Columbus and Central Ohio*

"Follow proven success methods." You may have heard that before. Well, Derek shares his success stories and tips in this amazing book! The neat thing about Derek is how he has achieved success in all areas of his life, and that speaks volume right there. He has learned from other successful people, taken action, kept notes along the way of his journey, and now has everything you need within this book to follow his proven success methods. Don't re-create the wheel. Start here by diving in and learn from one of the best

entrepreneurs I know. Grab a highlighter and go circle *Database*, and be sure to read that chapter often. This will be your greatest value especially when *you* are a value to your database. I will be forever grateful for meeting Derek and his wonderful, beautiful family! A faith-based man, Derek is highly focused, uplifting, energizing and eager to coach you to a higher level! Derek has taught me so much and he truly enjoys living out his purpose of inspiring and building into the lives of others. Just follow him, read his books, listen to his podcast, watch his videos, ask about his investments, coach with him…the list goes on. Anything you can do to learn from him will help you succeed and is sure to inspire you."
— *Shanna Pope, Cincinnati's Finest, KW*

"Derek is a true leader in the real estate industry, I would highly recommend not just the awesome books he has written, but to sincerely consider his coaching program. His heart is always to help others!"
— *Jennifer Vories, Realtor®, Mega Team Owner in Northern Kentucky*

"Derek's insight into a successful real estate career is dead on. His approach to optimizing your time and systems will help anyone who needs to be more productive in real estate sales. I've personally spent over 34 years actively selling real estate, selling over 2,000 properties and have used similar methods and strategies to have a successful real estate career."
— *Harold Powell, 34-year Realtor®, Ventura, California*

"Being a broker for over 14 years and now an International Real Estate Sales Trainer, Derek's *Seven Levers for Success in*

*Selling Real Estate* captured the essence of what is required to have a successful real estate career. I loved where he talks about leverage and how to obtain it for your business. This book has something for all levels of agents – beginners, mid-level and advanced. Easy to read, great content. I strongly recommended it."

— *Ifoma Pierre, Motivational Keynote Speaker, Trainer and Coach*

"I've built a number of businesses over the years and they have one thing in common: they all use levers to grow. It is impossible to build a business without that leverage. What you encapsulate in your book is something I never thought of: using the same application of levers to successfully grow a real estate business. I could not stop thinking how easy it would be for real estate agents who simply apply what they learn in this book to have a business that no longer controls them. As you know, I help a lot of top-producing real estate agents across the country generate more listings. In working with them, I've learned a lot about how they work. All of them seem to have one thing in common: they work ALL the time. I was impressed with how your book so clearly dissected what it takes to build a successful real estate business and get your time back. You've mastered the art of leverage, applying it to your real estate business, and that is phenomenal. If more agents applied what you write about in the book, I think they would see a strong increase in volume and a corresponding decrease in the time and effort it takes to produce it. And I congratulate you on that!"

— *Beatty Carmichael, Listing Marketing Expert and owner of AgentDominator.com*

"Do you want to succeed in real estate? I've been in the real estate business for seven years in Tampa Bay. Are you like me? Have you ever wanted to sit a top producer down for a couple hours and say, "Tell me how you are doing what you're doing?" Well, your prayers have been heard. In a weekend or less, you can hear from someone who has sold over 1,400 properties, over a 100 a year, and he is willing to tell you EXACTLY what he does! I would call this "A Realtor's® Handbook to Success" because it's concise, easy to read and without all the fluff. Thanks, Derek!"
— *Jeff Lewis, Realtor®, Tampa, Florida*

"This year marks my 40th year as a Realtor®. Over that period of time, a lot has happened in the real estate industry. Technology has changed how we do just about everything. But what we do really hasn't changed very much. That's right – what we do, as both fiduciaries and salespeople, really hasn't changed a lot. That's what Derek knows. That's why Derek teaches the skills and methods that are tried and true. In his calm, positive, determined, and inspirational way, Derek has broken through all of the clutter and distractions to show you the simple, understandable way to create your own successful real estate sales business. You are in very good hands. Now go do it!"
— *Reid Young, Realtor®, RE/MAX, 40 Years in Business*

"I like the book; it is short, but I learned a lot from it. You merged Kingdom entrepreneurship with what the world's system is. I am looking for a simple way to not just do my business by DOING, but also by BEING a Kingdom entrepreneur. Your book is a simple guideline on how to use leverage and make your business grow. I am not so much of

a reader, but I read your book from start to finish. Thank you for sharing your secrets."
— *Ira Wright, Realtor®, Santa Maria, California*

"I've had over ten years of making these same mistakes; I wish I had Derek's book when I started! His content is straight to the point and actionable. It's easy to read and was a good reminder to keep the business simple. It's all about consistent time on the right tasks that leads to success."
— *Jennifer Murtland, Realtor® and Real Estate Coach*

"This is a great resource for entry-level agents AND veterans. Lots of good reminders and antidotes to get agents involved in the "things" it will take to make it. This is a tough business and is not for everyone. I've listed and sold real estate for 38 years in Michigan, and this is useful information for anyone wanting to build their business. Use it to get ahead. This industry doesn't have a lot of good resources from the agents who are actually doing deals. "There are those who can, and those who do; be very careful who you listen too." In today's gotta have it now (GHIN) world, people want answers now. Derek's book gives lots of the answers real estate agents can use NOW. Get a copy and learn from his wisdom."
— *Mark Gleason, Author of 'Say It Sold,' Real Estate Developer, Realtor®, Michigan*

"Derek has an abundance mindset. That means he wants YOU to WIN, and in this book, he walks you through the practical aspect of winning in real estate."
— *Eric Newberry , Realtor®*

"Derek Tye's new book, *Seven Levers for Success in Selling Real Estate*, will change your business forever. If you have aspirations to turn your real estate sales job into a business, then this book is for you. Derek does an incredible job highlighting the levers that drive our real estate businesses to new heights. So what are you waiting for? Go read this book!"

— *Pres MiKissack, Regional Director, KW Ohio Valley Region*

"Derek Tye has masterfully laid out a strategic and comprehensive plan that will lead to success in the real estate business. His book is a must own for anyone looking for a simple, straightforward path to incorporate all of the methods one should use in building a real estate sales business. He has always been an innovator, especially having the foresight to leverage the Internet to drive leads successfully. His devotion to God and his family are admirable, and most agents who are feeling stressed or overwhelmed can learn by his example. By following the lessons he presents, anyone could achieve that perfect "work-life balance" that we all want so badly."

— *Ryan Rowley, The Ryan Rowley Group*

For additional resources and information on how to get Derek's scripts, checklists, listing presentation process and information about group coaching, go to
**www.KingdomRealEstateAgents.com.**

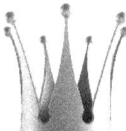

*Kingdom Real Estate Agents*

# *Table of Contents*

Foreword by Linda McKissack, 13
Acknowledgments, 15
Definition of a Lever, 17
Purpose, 19
Introduction, 21
Chapter One: Failing Forward, 25
Chapter Two: Why do you need leverage in real estate? 35
Chapter Three: Lever #1: People, 45
Chapter Four: Lever #2: Systems and Tools, 55
Chapter Five: Lever #3: Time, 63
Chapter Six: Lever #4: Listings, 73
Chapter Seven: Lever #5: Affiliations, 83
Chapter Eight: Lever #6: Database, 89
Chapter Nine: Lever #7: Content Creation, 97
Summary, 103
Resources and Routines, 107
Testimonials, 113
About Derek Tye, 118

# Foreword by Linda McKissack

Someone asked me the other day what I would do differently if I were starting my real estate career over. The answer is simple! I would understand how important learning and applying leverage to my business would be in my attempt to grow a big real estate business. I would start by learning the most important forms of leverage and immediately apply them in my business. Leverage in my life has shown up in big ways! It has created more freedom of my time, money and relationships; more than I would have ever dreamed. I can't imagine where my life would be today if I had tried to go it alone with no leverage. The only way to grow any business to a high level is to learn leverage.

The good news for you is you are reading this book. Derek's book is full of levers you need in the real estate business! If you want to know what levers are available to you as a real estate agent and what leverage you should apply in your real estate business, then start by reading this book. Next, immediately apply these lessons to create the biggest business possible. I encourage all of my agents to think big! Think with a mindset of abundance and limitless possibilities. There are many ways to sell real state – both with help and without. Personally, I would have appreciated a book like this when I was building my real estate business years ago. I firmly believe I would have gotten to 200 plus transactions a year a lot sooner and with a lot more freedom!

Let's get real. There are no shortcuts to success in life. There are lessons to be learned and processes to go through. I tell entrepreneurs to find someone who has gone before you and see what systems and tools that person has used. Success always leaves clues! It is up to us to learn to leverage our own time, money, and businesses to get us to where we want to be faster and with less carnage along the way. So, read and re-read this book, and then share it with your friends in the real estate business. Go ahead and dive in! Leverage the lessons Derek has already learned and is so willing to share.

Here's to your success in real estate!

— *Linda McKissack*, owner of a 7th-level real estate business, author of *Presentation Mastery for Realtors®* and co-author of *Hold: Buying and Holding Single Family Homes to Build Wealth*, co-host of the popular podcast "Everything Life and Real Estate"

# *Acknowledgments*

To God, for whom I exist to glorify. To my wife, Jessica, who I love dearly and who makes every day here on earth exciting for our family. To Montana, Maxwell and Parker Tye, my teenage sons who I am grateful to parent. To Gabrielle and Liliana Tye, my beautiful daughters who I am humbled to be a dad to. To my mom, who has always encouraged me that I could be anything I wanted to be. To my dad, who had strong faith in God and showed me how to live generously. To the many Realtors® who've helped me by reading this book and giving me advice on how to make it great. To the many giants in the real estate industry who have come before me that I can now stand on the shoulders of their books, trainings, systems and tools. To you, the reader, for taking a step of faith with your time and money to help yourself become a better agent and business owner.

# *Definition of Lever*

What is a lever?*

*Lever: a bar or handle which moves around a fixed point, so that one end of it can be pushed or pulled in order to control a machine or move a heavy object*

What is leverage?*

*Leverage: the action or advantage of using a lever*

What is leverage in the real estate business?

*Utilizing the time, talents and knowledge of people, growing teams, setting up systems and tools, time-blocking, developing your network and affiliations, and other strategies to expand your business, use less of your own time and avoid burnout.*

*Note: Taken from the Cambridge Dictionary.

# *Purpose*

The purpose of this book is to show real estate agents that they can:

- Live a fulfilling life in the real estate business without burnout
- Build a team, a company and a legacy through people, systems, tools and a big vision
- Help other people they care about build a big life, too
- Provide unlimited value and serve clients to the best possible level through an amazing career in real estate sales

These actions are accomplished only through a strong vision, great mentors, support and leverage. The leverage opportunities outlined in this book are not an exhaustive list, but levers I have found the most traction with. This book will serve real estate agents by providing a vision of what is possible, personal stories of success and failures and practical action steps to walk out a satisfying, sustainable career. Many giants in the real estate business have written amazing books on the topic of the sales, listing processes, lead generation, the concept of real estate as a business, and work-life balance. Instead of a 2,000-page manifesto in all things real estate related, I am simply inviting you to be a part of one real estate agent's journey of learning: mine.

# *Introduction*

When I was about 12 years old, I wrote a small guide about how to be a good salesperson. It was terrible and makes for a funny story now. My mom was my first and only reader of this book, until we found it years later and had a good laugh. She framed it a few years ago, and today it hangs in my office as a reminder that I am a "real" author. My mom always told me I would be successful someday, and deep inside I always knew she was right. What I couldn't quite grasp yet, was what my version of success would look like.

```
                  Derek's Tips
                      to a
                Successful Business

  1.  Always keep a smile and act nicely toward your
      victim.

  2.  Use manners when speaking to him or her, such
      as: "Miss," "Sir," "Gentlemen" and "Ladies."

  3.  Always have a good theme, and not just "I'm
      selling stuff." Use, "I have a lovely, . . ."
      "With a coupon for . . .," etc., if necessary.

  4.  The customer is always right.

  5.  Have a good cause to tell the customer, such as:
      "I need to buy my mom a present for her
      birthday," or "I need to make some money to
      take me through summer camp."

  6.  Admit your faults, "I'm new at this," or "I'm
      sorry for the inconvenience," or "These prices
      might be a little steep, but, etc. . . ."

  7.  Business before pleasure.

                              Derek Tye (age 12)
```

When I was young, I always imagined myself as the CEO

of a large company. So, when I finished high school, I decided I was going to graduate from college with a bachelor's degree in exactly four years (eight semesters). I did all the math, figuring the most efficient way to graduate with a bachelor's degree in business management was to maximize my credit hours each semester, taking between 12 to 17 credit hours. Although it's not uncommon for students to complete their degree in four years, I was doing it in addition to working 30 hours a week, getting married and being a homeowner. This time period, between 18 and 22 years old, proved to me that if I put my mind to something, I could make it happen.

As I reflect on that time in my life it seems like a distant memory, but at the same time feels like just yesterday. Although I did not end up becoming the CEO of a large corporation, I did become President of my own company: The Tye Group, my real estate sales team in Cincinnati, Ohio. More about my story in the next chapter.

A few years ago, I decided I wanted to write another "real" book. My first book was published in 2019 and has more to do with my faith journey as an entrepreneur than real estate specifically. This book you are reading now has been in my head for years, and I am happy to finally get it on paper. I have had some success in real estate and want to help other real estate professionals experience some of those same successes.

Success in business can be viewed through many different

lenses, and depending on who's looking, it might be either a good or bad thing. To me success has been great (with the counterbalance of my faith and family life), and I'm really excited to teach other real estate professionals how to recognize and experience true success. My main goal here is to help real estate agents achieve breakthrough in life and in business through *leverage*.

They say teaching is the best way to learn something, so the message in this book is really a reminder and lesson plan to myself. I'd like to invite you to share it along with me. Let's take this journey together, and I hope there is at least one small tip I have discovered and share in this book that will help make your life and those around you more successful.

As is only fitting, let's start out the success conversation with some of my failures in business.

# Chapter One

## *Failing Forward*

---

I grew up on the east side of Cincinnati, Ohio, in a suburb called Glen Este. Our school district consolidated after I graduated, so "Glen Este High School" is no more. If you were to look up that school right now, it doesn't even exist. Oh well. At least we have the memories of school spirit, team colors and hallway shenanigans.

I was born in 1976 to Gene and Jean Tye, and I always said I came from good "genes." My younger brother rounded out our family of four. We also had two half sisters and a brother from my dad's first marriage who occasionally lived with us. From early on, as young as I can remember, my dad worked many different kinds of jobs. Even though he had a successful teaching career in California when he and his first wife divorced, he moved back to Cincinnati where he was raised. It was here where he reconnected with my mom at a 15-year high school class reunion and married soon afterward.

My dad was unable to find a full-time teaching position in Cincinnati, but was able to be a substitute teacher and supplement his income with various sales positions. I even saw him take more humbling positions like driving a limousine for several years to help make ends meet. My dad passed away in 2000, but if there's one thing I remember about him, it was his dedication to generosity. He faithfully tithed to our church on all of our family's income and gave extra to charities he believed in. He would always take food to people who needed it and had a heart for widows, orphans and Native Americans.

My mom was the main breadwinner in our family. She helped shape my thoughts on hard work and discipline (even if she didn't love her 45-minute commute each way to work). She was employed by a big engineering firm and worked with the same group of people for about 40 years. Because of her amazing work ethic and almost never calling in sick, her supervisors took very good care of her. She was well respected. Although she wished she could have been a stay-at-home mom, she made the sacrifice to help the family pay the bills.

Our home was humble by some standards, yet we were happy, and I lived there my entire childhood. We had the biggest backyard in the area, making us the kid-magnet house. All the neighborhood kids came to play in our yard; the yard with the big trees for climbing and even a dirt volleyball court. I grew up digging holes, building tree houses, playing volleyball, baseball, driving remote control cars around the backyard, and making mud pits. That was a good life for us.

My parents decided to sell the house when I was 20. My wife and I got married young, bought the house from my parents and lived there another five years.

From a very young age I remember wanting to be a successful business person. Business and sales was in me. I started by participating in all the 1980's catalog sales opportunities – you know…stuff that you do to raise money for different things in elementary school and mail order catalogs found in the back of magazines. I even did this on my own, going from door-to-door, selling things and keeping track of the money with very detailed records. Charts and tables were my sales tools, even at this early age. Of course now we call those spreadsheets!

I remember going to my neighbors and having some fear that they were not going to want what I had to sell. Fears that they would answer the door and be mad crept up sometimes as I stepped onto their front porches. I also remember the smiles I got and the orders I took from people who were just *happy to help a kid out*. Specifically, I thought if I believed in what I was selling (a discount to a magazine the neighbor was probably already buying at the grocery store for a retail price) and stayed friendly, I would fill up that order form and get the money that I wanted.

Next, I decided to start a business washing hot wheels with the tiny car wash I got for my birthday. I never convinced any other kids to pay me for this, but it was one of my big ideas! Unfortunately, I didn't make any money.

One time my friends and I thought we would use our

awesome, 12-year-old, amateur skateboard skills and do a show. We would charge people $1 to come and watch. I promoted it with flyers we printed on our home computer door-to-door. Only our biggest fans (our moms) decided to come, and we didn't make any money. Unfortunately, I didn't make any money on that one either.

So for the next few years, I decided to focus on growing in skills and knowledge. During high school (and in college), I decided to join the school's drama and theatre program. I was the lead in one high school play and had minor roles in a couple others. Because of the plays, I met a lot of fun people, cultivated lasting friendships and made great memories. Theatre class also taught me how to memorize a script (which came in handy later for sales positions), how to block (stand in front of an audience when you are speaking) and to project my voice (without a microphone). It also gave me the confidence I needed to speak in front of a large crowd. I have since used these skills and experiences to emcee dozens of events ranging from Chamber of Commerce dinners to non-profit fundraisers, to church sermons and Vacation Bible School kids' events, to Board of Realtors® award nights. Thank you to the drama department at Glen Este High School and Northern Kentucky University.

A big part of my story is marrying my high school sweetheart, Jessica, and building an amazing life with her. We started dating when I was a junior in high school, and we were married in 1996, while I was a sophomore at

Northern Kentucky University (NKU). Jessica had just graduated from high school, so we were married very young by today's standards. Because of our ages, people told us we might be making a huge mistake, but we just felt that we were destined to be together. Boy, looking back I am so glad we took that chance. We have been happily married ever since and have five awesome kids and several businesses. This could have been a big miss in my life if I hadn't taken that risk early in my adult life.

After my graduation from NKU, I did my best to climb the corporate ladder while working for several Fortune 500 companies: Hasbro Toys, Cincinnati Bell and US Bank. I realized that as much as I loved being a businessperson, working for big corporations was not for me. I had all of these crazy ideas to change the products, add new product lines, revamp service methods, do radical marketing campaigns, and shake up the current business models at these companies.

While working at the Yellow Pages division of Cincinnati Bell, I remember coming up with an amazing idea. Think back to the year 2000 when all the companies were racing toward the new and exciting Internet. I was one of the 20-somethings who thought this *Internet thing* might actually take off. I proposed a radical idea: since our Yellow Pages company was (finally) rolling out new products to get traditional advertisers to expand their reach to websites and an online search directory, I thought it was only logical they would want to create some radical advertising for the consumers to see the value in using the online search too, in addition to the thick Yellow Pages book.

I pitched it to the decision makers in the marketing department so smoothly…

*Imagine a child using a thick Yellow Pages book as a booster seat. They have a laptop computer open, displaying our new "online" version of the yellow pages, for the next generation, and are showing their mom and dad the new technology.*

I thought this was brilliant, and actually I still think this was cutting edge! Unfortunately, the mentality of the management said that the child's *bum* on the sacred Yellow Pages would be insulting to the brand and image…so they said a big "NO" to my idea. So I didn't make or lose any money with this idea, but I probably lost some favor with the upper management!

In my next attempt at climbing a corporate ladder, I worked in the banking industry selling products to both consumers and businesses. Sadly, my frustration with corporate America continued. I remember one day, sitting at the closing table for a commercial purchase deal, seeing the real estate agent receiving a check for around $30K, while my bonus for the same efforts was about $350. *Three hundred and fifty dollars? Hmm, I am smarter than this.* Even though I earned a "respectable" salary, about $35K per year at the time, I thought I was better off taking my chances to earn commissions or profits instead. So I may have wasted a few good years in corporate America. Or I could use those experiences, relationships and understanding to work for me as an entrepreneur!

Shortly after this, I decided to step out of a salary job and become a full-time real estate agent. Since my wife and I had bought and sold a couple of houses early in our marriage (getting married and buying our first house at the same time), I already knew I liked the real estate business. A few years before this I also learned how to split/sub-divide land because of property we owned and split up. By sub-dividing a building lot off of the property, we made more money selling the vacant lot separately than we would have selling the house with an extra-big yard. At 25 years old I had arranged the survey, contacted the bank for a partial lien release, contacted builders in the area to see who may want to buy the lot, and arranged the title work – all of this on my own with no real estate license.

At age 28, with a fresh real estate sales license in hand, I quickly discovered plenty of basic training was available on how to stay out of legal trouble, but no real estate sales training matching the business model I was seeking: a team approach. There also were not a lot of real estate teams at the time to model after.

While working the corporate jobs, I learned a lot about technology, websites, using search engines and online advertising. I also learned a lot about leverage through people and systems. Because I went from a corporate setting directly into real estate, I quickly noticed sales team philosophies and approaches used in the corporate world were missing in the real estate sales world. The majority of real estate agents in 2004 were using very traditional methods to build and maintain real estate sales, including door knocking in neighborhoods, open houses, mailing postcards, hand-written letters, newspaper ads, bench ads, word of mouth, and BNI groups. And, they were all essentially doing this as individual agents, rarely using leverage and systems. Ironically, after all these years, many of these more traditional paths to real estate sales are still the norm!

When I got started in real estate in 2004, I decided to use technology most agents were not, including building an IDX (information data exchange) website. At the time, this website cost me a small fortune – about $10,000! I had to take out a second mortgage on my house to come up with the money, as a newly self-employed person with zero savings. It was a huge risk, but this website became something that set me apart from others in my industry and provided a ton of buyer leads for me to work with. There were so many leads in fact, it allowed me to employ and partner with other agents in my office and sell some of the leads to them. I also discovered that I could keep more traditional office hours if those agents worked with buyers and I worked with sellers. More on this concept later in the book.

This was my first big lesson in leverage! I learned how to

win through leverage; leveraging both systems and people. Everybody wins! Partners, clients, my family…

This may be shocking to some, but over the years I have spent over one million dollars on my real estate business. Hence, the "failing forward." The real path to success is a zig zag left and right and may come with bumps and bruises. Where did that million go, you may wonder? The money went to some unnecessary advertising, way too many websites, team promotions, sports sponsorships, payroll for administration, and even on some really dumb ideas that didn't work (some *really* dumb when I look back…). How do I view all seven figures of what I spent? As an excellent education! After all, that is what we really want from money we spend, right? We want to get the best education possible, and in my opinion experience is the best educator.

Over the last several years, I have been coaching the next generation of agents through in-person classes, coaching sessions, podcasts, my Roku network channel "Real Estate Experts," and on my YouTube channel. This book is another exciting way for me to share with you some of those insights and learning.

In real estate, there's plenty of time spent driving around, and I love to listen to audio books and podcasts in my car. The podcasts are from all over the world, and I love the diversity of cultures and points of view I get to hear. Doing this is part of a growth mindset I hope you can adopt.

(Especially in this business.) With all the failures and mistakes I have made, I have become much more coachable and willing to learn from others. If you are curious about what my favorite books and podcasts are, check out my resources list in the back of the book.

Fast forward after 16 years of failing forward, today we have a robust sales team that has produced, at the time of this writing, about 1,400 sales and over $300 million dollars in sold volume. I have won many awards over the years, including the "Realtor® of The Year" for the Southern Ohio Association of REALTORS®, and have served as a Director and President of our local chamber of commerce our local association of REALTORS® board.

The real estate business is constantly changing, and there are market cycles we cannot control. For the moment of time we have together in this book, let's focus on what we can control, direct and manage in order to build for the future. Build something that will be more likely to stand over time; something that will withstand the market changes and ups and downs of the economy.

I invite you to come on this journey with me. Let's discover together some insights gained from my failures and experience so far in the real estate business.

# Chapter Two

## *Why do you need leverage in the real estate business?*

---

The answer to this question is simple: because you don't want to fail! Question answered...end of chapter...just kidding! I won't end this chapter yet; there is much to discuss here. And, there are different levels of failure, right?

Let's put it bluntly. Most real agents quit the business in the first five years. That would be a pretty bad way to fail. On a popular blog site, Lab Coat Agents, they are saying that 75% to 85% of agents are out of the business completely by the fifth year. That is a real problem. Why does this happen? I believe a variety of factors contribute to this.

Let's start with why people get into this business to begin with. New agents see the big commission checks, flexible time schedule and glamorous "Million Dollar Listing" type of TV shows portraying a pretty amazing lifestyle. This does attract more and more people each year to become real estate agents and brokers.

I also believe some people have had negative experiences

with sub-par agents and have thought, "I could have done this myself better." And they could be right. When they do get a license though, they are not properly trained to be a business owner. This means learning skills they have not learned yet, like basic accounting, saving for your taxes, lead generation, scripts, customer service, delegation, and lead follow up skills.

There is another level of failure. You win those listing appointments, buyer appointments and sell a ton of real estate. You start working 60 to 80 hours a week and make a ton of sales. You don't watch your health and you get really sick. You don't watch your time with your spouse and start having relationship issues. You don't see your kids for dinner or activities, and they don't know who you are. You don't have time for your friends, and soon you don't have any friends. I actually think this is worse than failing out of the business completely. But that is for you to decide.

My goal with this book is to help you achieve sustainable success in the real estate industry. I will not be covering all the necessary areas new agents should be skilled in to start their careers. There are a lot of other resources available for that. My focus here is to help you gain leverage to succeed in both business AND life.

Again, here is the definition of the word leverage from the Cambridge Dictionary:

> *Leverage: the action or advantage of using a lever*

## What is a lever?

*Lever: a bar or handle which moves around a fixed point, so that one end of it can be pushed or pulled in order to control a machine or move a heavy object*

So what does this have to do with real estate? In the definition of lever, we see "to control a machine or move a heavy object." The machine is the real estate business. The heavy object is getting the business to work with you, not against you. Let's use an example. According to the National Association of Realtors®, the number one complaint of Realtors® in the last several years was "difficulty finding the right property."

Question: Is this a seller's or buyer's agent issue?
Answer: This is a buyer's agent's problem.

So, if you are spending a majority of your time, money and resources driving around with a buyer, trying desperately to get offers accepted, being outbid in a multiple offer situation, you are not using leverage. What leverage? That is for later in the book. See the chapter on *Listings*!

In addition to the type of real estate client you concentrate on (buyers vs. sellers), there are also other areas of this business that cause agents to either not make enough money and return to a job, or stay in this career and experience severe burnout. Why do agents get burned out?

After coaching agents on my team for over 15 years, I've watched agents get tired of managing multiple clients and answering calls all hours of the day, on weekends, holidays and on their vacations. I have been guilty of this myself over the years. One particular day when my kids were young stands out. We were vacationing at Disney World, yet I was trying to navigate through a difficult real estate sale back home. While standing in line for one of the rides, between text messages, email and phone calls, it was going downhill fast. The negotiation in this deal was so tense and stressful that it completely ruined my time with my family for that ride. Later I realized it was ruining my whole day. So what did I do? I made a mindset adjustment and put the phone away. I was definitely not using people or time leverage well that day, and we will discuss those topics more in later chapters.

If you do make it past the five-year mark selling real estate and you are making a good living (and see a bright future ahead in this business), you are probably still subject to the crazy schedule most real estate agents have. With late nights, working weekends, missing family functions, having your phone out at dinner, all of this can lead to damaged relationships and an unhealthy lifestyle. These symptoms can be helped with time blocking, some technology solutions, people leverage and some other solutions we will discuss in a later chapter.

One additional reason to learn leverage is to get your business unstuck at certain income level. "Scaling" is a term to describe increasing your business production without increasing your personal time required. For example, I have averaged about 40 hours per week working in and on my real estate business for most of my career, yet my income has significantly increased compared to when I started. How is this possible? Scaling your business is the best way to increase profits and not work yourself to death. This is also a topic we will dive deeper into later.

Imagine for a moment what life could be like…
- Helping people around you succeed and grow in life and business
- Helping your clients succeed at their goals
- Building a beautiful community around you
- Earning enough money, not only to bless you and your family, but having more than enough to help other people or organizations you care about without worrying about the time or money required to do so
- Being able to turn off your phone at dinner without worrying that you are missing a real estate deal that you need
- Being able to attend all your kids' activities without worry that you missed an appointment
- Being able to have time to go to church, exercise, go fishing, have lunch with a friend, volunteer during the day, or any other activity you can imagine

This is the life I want for you and your family (and you probably do, too). We can accomplish this through a strong vision and leverage to fulfill that vision.

About ten years ago, I started following Tim Ferris through his podcast and his book *The 4-Hour Workweek*. After reading the book twice, I had a revelation: I needed to work more efficiently. Hiring out for everything I could would allow me to focus on just the top 20% of the daily, income-producing activities. I then applied this thought to my personal life, my health and business. Two of Tim's subsequent books clarified it even more for me, *The 4-Hour Body* and *The 4-Hour Chef*. On his podcasts, I started listening to a bunch of gurus he would interview. Then, I bought their books, their programs, listened to their podcasts and almost joined one of their $25,000 per year mastermind groups. The idea of efficiency, building a big business, scaling my ideas fast and living life to the fullest in every area made me geek out! So I started with a vision, then looked for leverage opportunities in every area of my life. As I started achieving my goals, I then realized that maybe my goals needed to be defined and set with some of my other long-term dreams in mind.

Here are some questions I started asking myself. Take a moment to ask yourself these questions and write down your own answers:

- Do you have a vision?

- Do you know what your purpose here on Earth is?

- What is your big *why* and how do you figure that out?

- What is your unique value or gift?

- What are your core values?

- What are your business's core values?

- Do you know how to build a sustainable business that will outlive you?

These are some tough questions. I don't have a perfect answer for all of these for myself or for you. Every day I pray for answers. For me, I am passionate about many things: God, my wife, my kids, my friends, and my businesses. You probably have a similar list. Have you noticed there are seasons and time periods where one of those passions needs to take priority over the others? Gary Keller says there is no such thing as a "balanced life." I agree. One of life's big mysteries is to find a way achieve an optimal *counterbalance* in our lives as we have to let one thing take priority over another in different seasons of our life.

For example, I wanted to bring the journey and passion I had for building a profitable business in line with my faith journey. I knew there had to be a connection there, so I kept praying, reading, learning and exploring great authors, teachers and business coaches. I pursued a deeper relationship with God, and in return He guided me to discover true wisdom. That wisdom in turn helped me become a better businessperson, a better husband and a better dad. I can now put life into perspective through a different lens or frame of mind, which makes my business, my marriage and my relationship with my kids less stressful and more fruitful.

The process of bringing any dream, big or small, into reality is hard…at any age! There are many necessary steps and it can take a while. Remember, however, that your purpose needs to precede your plans. If you don't have the right purpose for your life, the plans will not be correct for your dream. It is like driving down a road without knowing where you are going. Sure, you can drive faster, but you still may be going in the wrong direction. The reason I put this section before the advice about specific leverage areas is that we all need to get crystal clear on *where* we want to go or else we'll never get there. All the strategies and tips I can present to you will not help you if you have not outlined your dreams, goals and things you want to accomplish.

So, let's assume for today you are on your way to discovering your purpose (or already have a clear idea of what that is). You have determined your core values. You know you don't want to be a statistic and fail out of the real estate business. You are committed to success and to your funding your big why. Now let's get to the first lever!

Why do you need leverage in the real estate business?

## *Key Takeaways:*

1. _____

2. _____

3. _____

4. _____

5. _____

# Chapter Three

## *Lever #1: People*

---

The problem with "People Leverage" is that people can be used, manipulated, taken advantage of or generally mistreated. When you hear about leverage through people, you may have thought something similar. I am not talking about using people for our own gain or any of these negative connotations. I am referring to working with people to achieve mutually beneficial results.

Partnering with others is what humans have been doing since the beginning of time. There are thousands of books outlining this concept, so I won't go into all those reasons. Here are a few areas in the real estate business that we will cover: Spouse, Coaches/Mentors, Buyer's Agents, Brokerage Office Staff, Administrative (or Virtual) Assistants, Transaction Coordinators, and Vendors.

*"Never forget that people are far more important than process, product or profit. This is not a permit for them to be a low producer, but on the contrary when your people know that you value them above the other p's, they are connected to the reason you started your business in the first place. Those people will outperform, out produce and most importantly outlast."*
— *Eric Newberry, Realtor®*

Before we go through these roles, let's talk about what you have to do before you start involving other people in your life's work. First, dream big and write down those ideas. Second, establish a vision to achieve that dream. Third, put plans in place to map out your path. Fourth, ask yourself who you need in your life to walk out this plan. Fifth, show those people your dream, your vision, your plans, etc., and show them who else will be involved. If they agree to work with you to accomplish that dream, you are on your way!

Walt Disney created a vision map for his future empire in 1957 before Disneyland, Marvel Comics or ESPN. This vision was huge and took a lot of dreaming to make it become reality. He cast such a big vision that others got excited to join him. Someone could start as a base-level employee and grow with his company in any of the multitude of business units.

How big is your dream and vision? I followed Disney's example and built my own dream map of my future empire. Once per year I've updated the map, and it keeps getting more specific. Some of these business goals have actually come to life. As I am interviewing new agents or office administrators to work with me in my company, I always show them the Disney map and my map. I show them how our company is going to grow beyond what I can even think of. It's also important for them to know how I view my hiring process: I am hiring future CEOs (not just the position they have applied to).

How big is your vision? Is it big enough to attract other winners to be a part of your organization? Let me ask you this. Would YOU rather join an organization with higher pay and lower advancement opportunities or lower pay with higher opportunities for the future? To me the choice is easy! And I want to attract others who think the same way.

Before you hire your first person, the first area we all need help and support in would be an understanding spouse. I would recommend getting your spouse (if you have one) or best friend to begin this journey with you. They should know you better than anyone. They will also know how a decision you are about to make is going to not only effect you personally, but also your family, health and finances. You can discuss it together and will have to live with the decision you both jointly make.

For me personally, I also know that my wife, Jessica, has great intuition and discernment when it comes to people. She can usually pick up on someone's true motives and character better or faster than I can. She may say something like, "I am getting an uneasy feeling about that person, so just take it slow in that business relationship." By the way, she has never been wrong on that! I highly recommend having a spouse to support you like Jessica does for me!

If you don't have a spouse (or if you do and want double the help), seek out a trusted friend. Please start investing in great friendships *now* long before you need the critical advice they will provide. Start building into their life and they will build into yours. As little or big decisions come up, bounce them off your friend and get some good, honest feedback. I have had friends tell me to back off some of my big business decisions and not to step in that direction. The advice ended up being very timely and accurate. I had another friend tell me to focus on my real estate business when what I really wanted to do was just work on the new, flashy side hustle I dreamt up. That was good advice too. So it just took me a while longer to write this book as I worked my business!

Third, on the must-have people in your life list, is a business coach or mentor. These are people you really look up to and who probably have more experience than you at whatever the topic is. These people have achieved victories in areas that you aspire to. Has this person climbed a mountain, build a successful business, written a book, won a fishing tournament? Whatever you are trying to achieve, there is probably someone in your community who has already done that.

I always appreciate the advice of a coach or mentor. For the last several years I have had business coaches, and each time we connect I learn more about myself and have someone who can point out my blind spots. Specifically, a good coach does all of these things and more:

1. Helps you discover what you really want
2. Helps you get clarity on how to quantify that goal

3. Helps you get clarity on how to achieve that goal
4. Gets you encouraged to do the work
5. Holds you accountable
6. Repeats the process over and over!

When you know your vision, you then get a purpose and a plan. You have your spouse or best friend for support. You have a mentor or coach in place for success. Now you need to get strategic about adding working partners to your world. When you are growing your organization or team, I would highly recommend sticking with the old adage: "hire slow, fire fast!" Take your time and really interview someone multiple times. See what they are like on different days, different times of the day.

Have other team members interview the person as well. You want this to be a good business AND cultural fit inside your organization. I let candidates know that there will be several rounds of interviews and that it needs to be a unanimous decision on my team. The culture on our team is more important than getting a new hire in quickly. I also encourage you to fire fast if the person isn't working in the first 90 days. We create a probationary period for every new hire. We can see if we are a mutual fit for each other. This comes with specific 30, 60 and 90-day progress report steps.

If you don't have a team yet and this is your first hire, I would recommend having a coach or mentor also meet with the person. If this absolutely cannot be done in person, then I would at least ask for a video interview to be done. Body language is too important and non-verbal communication is critical to pick up on.

I really like the book, *The Millionaire Real Estate Agent*, by Gary Keller. About ten years ago, I read it as I worked on scaling up my real estate team. He talked about when to hire for strategic positions, such as a buyer's agent, administrative assistant/transaction coordinator, listing specialist, etc. What I have learned from 15+ years of doing this is pretty close to what he outlined in the book.

Most agents wanting to scale up their business will start by finding another agent in the office and call them their buyer's agent. This sometimes works, but mostly does not. This often leads to a team that is really a partnership between two agents, but as soon as one of the agents decides to split off, there is no longer a team. What I have found that works better is for an agent, who is on pace to sell at least two homes a month, hires a transaction coordinator first. This individual helps the agent with the immediate needs of transactions – to get the paperwork side of the business done while the agent is able to concentrate on key activities for success.

My recommendation is to start with the Transaction Coordinator first, then add a buyer's agent second. A buyer's agent typically works for a rainmaker (an agent who is consistently getting business) and takes the extra business the main agent does not want (or have time for).

When you start hiring, use this phrase and repeat after me: *Hire Slow, Fire Fast.* You need to take your time, set up multiple interviews, review resumes and actually call the references. This is critical!

In my scenario, starting a team in 2004, one of my priorities was to set up a time block where I could work a more traditional 8:00 am to 6:00 pm timeline. Being home for dinner, available to participate in the kids' activities at night and on the weekends and attend church on Sundays is important to me. I hired my wife to help be the behind-the-scenes administrator setting up showings, running searches on MLS, wrapping up files after closing and other important functions.

Next, I found another agent in my office who was great with buyers, had an amazing personality, was very driven, but had my opposite needs for a schedule. She had kids in the home during the time when her husband worked (during the day) and wanted to be productive outside the home working evenings and weekends. So I hired my first buyer's agent, Debbie! She was a great partner and we worked for seven years together like this. My next hires were buyer's agents over the years, and I have always kept my position as the main listing agent and team leader.

Over the years, I learned I also needed other positions in my business life. I partnered up with several real estate investors, a lender, a title company, a few home inspectors, two great photographers, an excellent mover, a business coach, a handyman, a new construction builder and remodeler, a roofer, a radon mitigation specialist, and other various vendors. Building a great relationship with all these partners has been the best leverage of all. I coach my agents and other business owners to ask the most important question when they run into a problem. You don't ask *How* or *What*, you ask *WHO*. Who should I be talking to, to help me solve this issue? Or who would know the person I should be talking to? This is critical in our path to understanding how to create leverage through people and be on our way to a more successful life!

Ultimately we want to succeed *with* other people. We want to win together. We want others to reach success. And, it is fun to be a part of that journey. To end this chapter, here's a quote from a top agent in the country. It will help give you a great perspective on putting this "people lever" to work in your business:

*"Your BIG WHY should somehow be connected to your desire to bless others in your company as you have been blessed. Example: to provide the coaching, systems and environment so that my people and their family never have to say no to something they deserve a yes to. That's my BIG WHY. True success in business is found when your people reach their goals. A leader's job is to put others on stage."*
*— Ricky Cain*

*Key Takeaways:*

1. _____

2. _____

3. _____

4. _____

5. _____

## Chapter Four

# *Lever 2: Systems and Tools*

---

Increasing productivity and gaining efficiencies while running your business is vital. When other agents are doing things manually or one at a time, you can be scaling, growing and servicing multiple clients. So what are the best systems and tools to create massive leverage in your real estate business?

**MLS**
Let's start with the Multiple Listing Service. If you are a real estate agent, you should get very familiar with the way your local MLS system works. Many offer features like map searches, address searches, daily hot sheets with new listings, MLS Portals for client automation, built-in showing scheduling, access to reports and tools for analysis, and much more. Don't take this tool for granted. My advice is to take a class at your local board on how to use this tool and learn all the features. You will not regret it.

**Automatic Saved Searches**
Whether you use the saved search system built into your local MLS or a tool through your company's website, I highly recommend this for your buyers. When you set up an automatic search, you automate the process for sending

new listings to your buyers. Clients see new listings that match their search criteria the moment they come on the market. It may seem obvious to use a tool like this, but you would be surprised how many agents never set up one of these for their clients.

Let's say your buyer is looking for at least 3 bedrooms, 2 full baths, 2 car garage and a specific school district. And the price range up to $350,000. You set up this search, add the client's email address, and boom. That is it. The client gets the emails with new listings and you are not at the computer every day looking for more listings for your buyer. As they come on the market, you can also be copied on the new listing emails. If you see one pop up that you especially love for your client, you can call them directly and let them know right away. This has worked wonders for me over the years and it is one less thing I need to worry about.

**Email System**
This is another obvious tool, but how you use email can make the difference between being just another agent or a Rockstar Agent. Here are a few tips I have learned.

Less is more: First (the hardest one, and don't laugh), try to keep less than 100 emails in your inbox. If you have more than that, your brain can not sort out what is what, everything gets mixed up and you have a difficult time locating important messages. Busy executives use this strategy and I have been successful with it for a few years.

How is this possible when I currently have multiple businesses, 22 listings as of today, several employees, volunteer organizations, and lots of spam? Here is how I keep less than 100 emails in the inbox:

1. I make quick decisions to either delete, file in individual files for storage, keep in my inbox for later or delegate to a vendor, administrative assistant, agent on my team or someone else to take care of.
2. If I keep it in my inbox for later, I use that like a "to-do" list and double check once a day to see what I still need to do myself. If I find myself going back to the same items over and over, I go back to step one and either delete, file or delegate.
3. I use two spam filters. One filter is set up through unroll.me, and I can set that to show me all my emails that are not necessarily junk once a day; emails like news from my favorite restaurant, newsletters I've signed up for, etc. The second filter is through my Gmail service. If I flag something as junk, it sends it to a spam filter. Every now and then I get something that goes to that folder accidentally that I really needed. Otherwise, it really cuts down on the clutter.
4. The coolest thing I do is hire my Director of Operations (administrative assistant for my team) to go in once or twice a day and filter out my emails using the same system. So here is an example: my admin looks for spam, marks it as such and deletes it. She finds an email asking me to send closing instructions to a seller. She forwards that to our team's Transaction Coordinator to

fulfil that request. She sees a reminder about my upcoming doctor's appointment and puts it on my calendar. You get the idea. I highly recommend this and it will make you more productive like other executives. Don't forget to learn more about leverage through people in Chapter 3.

**CRM**

A customer/client relationship management system is software (either on your computer or on the cloud) that organizes your database and helps you stay in touch with them. What makes a great system? The system needs to be relatively easy to use and must have good technical support when you run into problems. You should easily be able to add new contacts (daily) as you do your lead generation and be able to sort and find them quickly for your daily lead follow up. The system should also have the ability to send out some kind of automated newsletter or mass email to your database. Most importantly, the system you choose has to be something you will actually use every day. Even if you use a spreadsheet, email or some other basic service, the best CRM is the one you will actually use.

**Online Storage**

There are many systems out there for storing photos, contracts and other files. I like to use Google Drive and Dropbox. These are two of the most popular ones, and I have not had any trouble with either one. Many real estate offices are going to all digital files and eliminating paper storage. After doing this business for over 15 years, I have a whole storage building full of office files and transaction files. There are thousands of files in there! We are now in the process of only keeping the last 12 months in hard copy format and everything else will be stored on the cloud.

**Contract Management**
There are quite a few options out there to use for managing contracts and documents. Dotloop has a popular system. Some prefer Skyslope. Keller Williams has its own contract system that just launched. If you are with a smaller company, you have more control over which system to use. Some larger companies require agents to use a certain system. The efficiency of having clients sign documents electronically has created a huge time savings (leverage) in this business. We used to run around town collecting wet signatures or use fax machines (if you could find one). Now on our phones we can create a document and have it signed within minutes. When you are dealing with intense contract negotiations, this is amazing! It also saves me thousands of miles on my car each year.

**Social Media**
Facebook, Twitter, Instagram and other social media outlets can be fantastic to use for leverage. Let me explain...

The most important time activity for a real estate agent is lead generation. If you leverage social media in the right way, you can communicate with far more people than you can one at a time. This is more efficient, but may not be more effective than an old-fashioned phone call or an almost old-fashioned text message. If you post strategically about your business and don't make people cringe when they see your posts, you can stay in front of your ideal audience. Many social media platforms also have a direct messaging feature to send direct messages to people you want to stay in touch with. Many times I don't have the phone number or email address of someone, but I can direct message them on Facebook. This is an efficient and effective way to reach them.

**Workflow**

What happens when…? This is a question you should know before it happens, and you should have a process in place for all real estate sales scenarios. Let me give you a quick list:

- What happens when I get a call into the office?
- What will my admin say?
- How do we set up appointments on my calendar?
- What script do I use at a listing appointment?
- After the client signs a listing agreement, what happens next on the team?
- What is our listing advertising strategy?
- What websites do we use to advertise?
- Who inputs the info into all these systems?
- Do we have a photographer and when do they take the photos?
- What happens when we get an offer?
- What happens when we have an accepted contract?
- Who handles the inspection requests, negotiation and

resolution?
- What is our process from inspection, to appraisal to closing?
- What do we do for the client at and after closing?

These are just a small sample of questions you should be asking yourself before the needs arise.

**Checklists**

This is really simple and obvious, but use checklists in your business. We have one for before we list a house (preparing for the listing presentation), a checklist for once we have a signed listing agreement through pending status, a contract (to purchase) to closing checklist and others. Some of this has been learned through trial and error and some has been though borrowing from other top agent teams generous enough to share their wisdom with me and our team. At the back of this book we have additional resources on this topic.

**Scale and Sustainability**

Systems and tools are good in the moment, but are better when used over time. As you build and develop all of these systems, please keep future sustainability in mind. As my friend Ricky Cain says, "When building out systems and processes, build them to be scalable and to where you intend the company to be 20 years from now." This goes back to vision. Where do you want to be in 20 years? Work backwards to today and start building systems that will last.

## Key Takeaways:

1. _____

2. _____

3. _____

4. _____

5. _____

# Chapter Five

## *Lever 3: Time*

---

Why do highly successful people always get more done? My mom always told me, "if you want to get something done, give it to a busy person." This adage holds mostly true. As long as the busy is also productive. Being "busy" all the time does not correlate directly with being "successful." So we don't want to make that assumption. Being a master of time is more important than being busy.

**How do you start your day?**
One thing I have learned in my career is that super successful people wake up earlier and get more done by lunch than most people get done all day and night. Why is that? I think the biggest time lever is *priority*. There is an excellent book by Gary Keller called, *The One Thing*. If you haven't done so already, read this book. Listen to it on audible. Then do it a few more times. As a team, we have even read this book together (like a book club) multiple times. The principles in that book have shaped some of my guiding principle on time leverage. I would summarize the main learnings from the book as this:

1. Success is built sequentially, not all at once. The first domino matters the most.
2. Not all activities you spend your time on matter

equally.
3. Discipline is a result of habit.
4. Willpower is a finite resource.
5. A balanced life is a lie – you must have counter-balance.
6. Going Big in life is the only way to live.
7. Focus your efforts by asking this important question: what is the one thing I can do, such by doing it, that everything else will be easier or unnecessary?

**Do the most important things first.**
Keller and other authors have picked up on a very important time lever: the 80/20 Principle. This is also called Pareto's Law. It was named after the Italian economist Vilfredo Pareto in 1895. He discovered that 80% of the wealth was owned by 20% of the people. Likewise, 80% of your business comes from the top 20% of your clients.

Brian Tracy, in his book called *Eat That Frog*, also encourages us to do the same prioritization on our "to-do" lists and our daily activities. If you find out what the most important tasks are, the ones more significant than any others, you need to do those first. In other words, *Eat That* (most important) *Frog* first. The concept is great, and I love that book too. If we spend our day knocking off all the easy items on our list, we may avoid the most impact-producing, more challenging activities; the vital activities that ultimately lead to a better life.

In the real estate business, as a salesperson, you really have five key activities to focus on each day. These have been adapted from classes I have taken at Keller Williams Realty.

**Five Key Daily Activities:**
1. **Lead Generation.** Phone calls, door knocking, post cards, letters, Facebook ads, etc., for new business.
2. **Lead Follow Up.** Once you have made contact, you have to keep reaching out regularly until they buy.
3. **Practice Scripts.** Practice what you will say to a prospective buyer/seller to get an appointment or in negotiations.
4. **Go on Appointments.** Go on listing appointments, show homes to buyers, networking events, meals.
5. **Negotiate Contracts.** Once you have secured a prospect, write and negotiate the deal.

If you focus on these five key activities consistently every work day, I believe you have a much higher probability of success than agents who don't do these activities daily. If you do, two distinct results will occur. First, you will make more money. Second, you will choose to spend your work time more wisely (productivity), which should allow you more time with your family. Back to that in a minute.

So how do you focus on the most important priorities? Here are some tips:

1. Start with your big dream, vision and goals. Then, work backwards to determine what you need to get done this

year, this month, this week, then in the next day.
2. Based on #1, plan out the night before what are the top few key activities to get done the next morning. Don't wait until morning to figure it out.
3. Create a bunker until you get those things done. It might be a quiet office with the door closed. You may have to put your phone on "do not disturb." And turn off your email notifications. You might have to put snacks, water and coffee in the room so you don't leave. And, stay off of social media until you are finished. Facebook can wait.

**Don't be *that* guy.**
I remember hearing a story years ago. A man kept coming home late from work every night, missing dinner, spending just a little time with his family, and then opening up his laptop again and working until bedtime. One night, the son said to his mother, "Why does Dad always come home late and work after dinner?" His mother says to the little boy, "Your dad has a lot of work and is always behind." The little boy then says, "At my school there are kids that never get their work done and they make arrangements for them. They should put Daddy in the SLOW LEARNER'S CLASS."

I wonder how true that is. They say the definition of insanity is to do the same thing over and over and expect a different result. If we see patterns in our life like this, we need to make changes. Our family does deserve it. Early in my real estate sales career, I desired to spend as much time with my wife and kids as possible, but didn't know how to balance work and home life. My wife and kids were usually available after work or school and before bedtime.

As I started my career, I found that most Realtors® and agents worked 9:00 am to 9:00 pm, seven days a week. The reason most people work these hours is that making lots of money can be addicting and fun, and most aggressive business owners like to work *a lot*. Maybe you can relate! There is also one other reason. A lot of us have a hard time telling clients "no" and setting boundaries around our personal and family life.

A lot of these same people have not set time blocks for other important things. For example, if a healthy body is important to you, you may want to time block 30 minutes of fitness training three times per week. If your family dinner time is important to you, you may want to time block your schedule to get home by 6:00 pm. If your faith or spirit life is important to you, you may want to block out every Sunday morning for a worship service.

**Seasons of Life**
During the first year of selling real estate, my wife and I had to endure a season of sacrificing our family time together in order to run buyers around town showing homes. This was a reality until our business was more financially stable. For at least a year or so, I met clients whenever and wherever they wanted. I tried my very best to make all the sporting events and family parties too. I did

have to make that time sacrifice for a while until I was able to hire administrative employees and partner with buyer's agents to help with the client load.

I also know that there are seasons for harvesting business in different industries. In our real estate industry, spring and summer time are the busiest, as people want to move when kids are out of school. This also means we may have to take on a larger workload and meet people earlier or later than our normal schedule would tell us to operate. We then have to counter balance those times when things are slower, like around Thanksgiving, Christmas and New Year, when the calls from clients to list their homes slows down. Sometimes I need to remember to take a little time for myself and my family to compensate for those late nights at the office in the summer time and not stress out if I don't have a lot of clients at that time.

**Accidental Success**
One of my accidental success stories was when I created a real estate website that got me more leads than I had time to work myself. Remember, this was way back in 2004 when today's high-quality, professional-looking websites displaying MLS listings from other brokers didn't really exist yet. I got this idea to create a one-stop portal for all the listings in my hometown of Cincinnati, Ohio…all 15,000 listings on my website vs. just the two I had personally listed.

What was the result? We had scores of real estate buyers

contacting us through our website; buyers we had never met who wanted information on homes we were not the listing agents for. This is pretty much how Zillow started their business several years later.

These "leads" needed people to show them homes in the evenings and on the weekends. Because of the large number of leads coming in, I was able to ask other agents in my office if they wanted to run some buyers around for showings. I also asked them to split the commission. They wanted the leads; I needed the time. We split the money! And it allowed me to be home during those hours when the family was home and available. It was a perfect fit for everyone!

**What Happened Next…**
The indirect result was a sales "team" that I still run 16 years later! The abundance of leads led to more people who I could partner with. The income from those sales allowed me to hire an additional assistant to do all the paperwork, creating more leverage of my time and of my agents. I was then able to work more with sellers, on the listing side of the business, which makes it easier to control my time. Buyer's agents showed the properties and I was able to be home for dinner most evenings by 6:00. Rarely have I missed a game or practice all these years. Additionally, partnering with others has allowed me to serve many more real estate clients than I could have alone, and our team has now sold over 1,350 homes.

Over the last 16 years of being a full-time entrepreneur, I have been invited to do volunteer work with various organizations. Since I was prioritizing my working time, I had gotten pretty efficient in delegation of my time and selling over 100 homes per year without working more than 40 hours per week on average. I had a few interests outside of work, so the next logical step was to start volunteering for some organizations I liked.

Serving alongside some amazing people during that time was a wonderful experience. For my local board of Realtors®, I went from committee member to chair, to Vice President, to President, and onto the board of directors. Simultaneously, I went from Director to Vice President, then to President of our city's chamber of commerce. At the same time, I was also on the leadership team for our men's ministry at our church. Did I mention we were also hosting a small group at our house during the same timeframe? Of course, this is in addition to all the activities my wife was involved with. Having five kids, a loving wife, a business, close friends, sports activities, and church activities makes for a full life. After doing all of this for over ten years, I decided I wanted to write a book and do some coaching and speaking. Saying "no" to all these other things was pretty hard.

One of the time levers I used in this season of transition was to start paring down the activities I was involved in outside of work. So I stepped down from the chamber, the board of Realtors®, the leadership team at our church and some other regular volunteer activities. This was a five-year process, which has led to some time savings and the ability to write two books this past year. In the future as I move back into some regular volunteer roles, I have a new perspective on how to not let the volunteering get out of hand again.

In summary, we need to be masters of our time. Start with your first few hours and become really amazing at mastering your day before noon. When your willpower and energy is at its best, do your highest-priority work – your lead domino that turns your goals into reality. At the end of this book, I have included some daily affirmations and goals that I read out loud before each workday. Feel free to customize this list to help you get your day started as well.

## Key Takeaways:

1. _____

2. _____

3. _____

4. _____

5. _____

# Chapter Six

# *Lever 4: Listings*

---

If you don't get anything else out of this book, I hope you at least learn this one big leverage tool. I am going to give it some space to breathe here on its own...

Listings = Leverage!

Now, I am going to break up this chapter up into two sections. First, I will show you why you should concentrate your efforts on seller listings instead of buyer clients. Second, I will show you how to actually get more listings and increase your efficiency and profitability.

**Part 1: Why concentrate on taking seller listings?**
Let's start with a story. Years ago I listed a home for a builder client. To this day, I am still selling homes for him. But back to the story...one day a client called me, getting my number off of the FOR SALE sign in the listing's front yard. This nice couple lived about two miles down the street. The listing was a nice, new, custom-built, one-story home. They decided to buy it. Then, I asked them what they were going to do with the home they currently lived in. They wanted to sell, so I took that listing. Soon afterwards, I sold that house too.

The next-door neighbor to that house saw me sell this home. She called me and asked me to sell her home. She also bought a condo with my help after her home sold. Then, she referred me to another neighbor a few streets away. I then sold that home. That client then did another sale with me not long after. Another neighbor on the street saw me sell those two homes. She was getting a divorce. I then sold her home. Next, both the husband and the wife each bought different homes with my help.

Do you see this? Each listing spawned another piece of business. I can retrace a lot of my sales over 15 years like this.

Why the story? Here is the summary. When you list a house, you have several points of leverage. First, you get the advertisement of the real estate sign. When neighbors drive by, they see your company, your face and your name. Just make sure it sells relatively quickly or that sign can work against you. Second, you get to leverage that listing on your social media. You get to let everyone know you are doing business in that area. Next, you get to receive the buyer calls off of the sign and the advertisements you put out. This should be as good as the listing commission plus some. Many times the buyer also has a house to sell. Also, you get the listing side of the commission no matter who sells the home.

If you have a good listing (in good condition, priced well, with a great location), it should sell and you will win either way. As the listing agent, if it goes into multiple offers, you are guaranteed the sale. If you are representing a buyer in a multiple-offer situation, you only have a small chance that your client will win out.

Here is the bonus that most agents don't think about: time leverage within the listing lever. Let me explain. When most buyer's agents are running around town showing properties and making offers, you have time leverage. You can be home for dinner, make the soccer game, see your mom for lunch, you name it. That is one of the best reasons to have listings.

If you truly do a great job on selling this house, you will want to leverage that sale to the neighbors, of course, to earn more business in that neighborhood. Make sure to put a "Sale Pending" sign out and then a "SOLD" sign out where allowed by your local laws. This is a great way to advertise that you are the best!

Another great reason to take listings is to attract and retain top buyer's agents on your team. I give my agents first right to hold the houses open on the weekends and give them the buyer calls that come off of the sign calls and advertisements. If you ask potential buyer's agents what is most important to them about joining a team, most will say LEADS! Having more listings will help you attract better talent.

Now, don't forget open houses. Many buyers come into the

home as an unrepresented buyer and need an agent to help them navigate the complicated process of purchasing a home. Most do not buy the first house they see. If you can educate them and give them a vision of how the process could go, you may just win over another buyer. There are no limits to how many buyers you can pick up in one open house.

Another amazing benefit is the income opportunity of both sides of the sale. In our town when we get both sides of a real estate sale, we call it a "Double Dip" commission. I know this is not the norm in some real estate markets, but I do enjoy serving both the buyer and seller in some cases. Check with your local broker about rules regarding this.

**Part 2: How to take more seller listings.**
Now you are *absolutely convinced* that you should prioritize your lead generation toward listings vs. buyers, right? Your first question may be, "So how can I take more seller listings?" Great question!

**Get in front of as many sellers as possible.**
Your first goal needs to be to get in front of sellers. You can do this by farming a neighborhood with postcards over time, advertising in a local magazine, sponsoring events there, calling expireds, calling for sale by owners, circle prospecting (after a past sale, for an open house or for a potential buyer), or other methods. The key is to focus on a neighborhood or area where you want to do business in and keep working that area. Some newer agents choose too

large of an area and cannot keep up with the regular contacts necessary to dominate that market. Consistency over time is more important than a temporary advertising campaign.

**Use scripts.**
If you are not already, start using a script. There are a hundred different listing scripts out there from different real estate gurus. Which one is the best? The one you use! Practice your script and feel comfortable delivering it with people on the phone before you use it on a potential client. The more fluid and "normal" you sound, the more comfort and trust you will build up. Knowing the right thing to say to get an appointment is half the battle.

> *"When you LISTen they LIST, and when you talk they walk. You'll be paid in direct proportion to the quality of the questions you ask."* — Mark Gleason

**Do your research.**
Before you go to the listing appointment, make sure to thoroughly research your clients' home, the recent sales comps, what homes are pending sale and what the pricing looks like for other homes for sale nearby. If there are vacant active and sale-pending homes in the neighborhood, and if you have time, do a personal tour of those. If you do this and can demonstrate expertise at the listing appointment, this will win you huge leverage with your potential listing client. They want to feel confident that you know the competition and area at a high level. You will

also need to know what other listing websites think about their value. I pull up all the popular listing websites, like Zillow, and use those values as part of the perception of what a potential buyer will think their home is worth.

**Have a hook.**
In our business in the Cincinnati area, there are over 6,000 real estate agents, give or take. There were about 23,000 homes sold in the last year. So if every agent were to get their fair share of listings, they would end up with about four each. Our team of four agents listed 60 homes this year, or about four times the average. So what sets us apart and gives us our "unfair share" of listings? You need to have a hook or a unique value proposition.

When you are face to face with a client, you need to know what sets you and your team apart from the average agent. You should know your average sale price, average days on market and other key stats compared with the market average. Hopefully your numbers are much better!

**Have a great listing presentation.**
This goes along with scripts, but just showing up and "winging" it will not cut it unless you get lucky or the client is not interviewing other agents. Find an agent in your office who knows what they are doing and has proven success in listing homes. Ask them to share what they use as a listing presentation. Do this with several seasoned agents, and then try and come up with your own version. (To learn more about the specific listing scripts my team

uses, please refer to our coaching program information at the back of the book.)

*"If you are going to be in the business of meeting and exceeding your clients' expectations, you have to find out what those expectations are. You have to move to a consultative approach to find out what is most important for them in a transaction. Most of the time when there is a problem, it is because of a miscommunication about what was expected. We have found that the best way to find out what is expected is just to ask!"*
*– Jim and Linda McKissack*

**Give excellent service.**
One of the best ways to secure listings is to get referrals from your current and past, highly-satisfied clients. If you provide excellent service and provide tremendous value over time, clients will want to talk about you and refer you to their friends, family and neighbors. Just think about it…after you have been to a great, new restaurant and had an unbelievable experience, you want to tell your inner circle all about it. You should strive for the same level of service.

**Have a great support system.**
A system is a good way to understand this. If you do not have a great support system, you are on your own and will have a hard time with sustainable success in the real estate business. Some examples of our listing systems are:

1.  System for preparing for the listing presentation

2. System for having all the contract paperwork signed
3. System for after the listing contract is signed at the office (file creation, ordering signs, etc.)
4. System for pre-home sale preparation and staging
5. Professional photography
6. Marketing process
7. Listing input
8. Open house process

This is not a complete list, but it gives you a look into a top real estate team's systems and what we do. We take listings very seriously and want to make sure our clients know it and see it.

**Close**

I either get the potential listing client to sign a listing agreement on the spot or schedule a follow up call or appointment to do so. I will then follow up with that potential seller every week until they list with me or ask me to stop calling. After three months I will follow up with them every month; every month forever to see if they are ready to sell. Sometimes the seller sells three months later. Sometimes it takes three years. At times I have also been disappointed to hear that the seller has decided to take my advice on staging and pricing, but then sells it "For Sale By Owner." And yes, that hurts! No one likes doing something for nothing, especially in a business context, but it happens.

Despite disappointments at times, here is a big life lesson I have learned in business: sometimes I am rewarded with revenue, sometimes I am rewarded with life experience. Either way I *win*. That is part of my mindset every day. I have to be willing to see no monetary reward for the opportunity to do business with a new client and simply build a new relationship. Don't stop prospecting for new listing business. It will pay off in the long term!

**The Fun Part**

Once you start really building up a reputation in your community or neighborhood, most sellers will know your name. They will really want your opinion about the marketability of their home before it hits the market. This plays out as FOMO: fear of missing out. They don't want the top Realtor® to not weigh in on the value of their home. So, this is when it gets fun. You get the calls that go something like this.

*Caller: "Hi my name is Bob. We live at 123 ABC street. My wife and I have noticed that you have sold a bunch of homes in our neighborhood and we are going to be selling ours this spring. When would **you** have time to come out and look at our place so we know what we need to do to get it sold?"*

Do you think this is realistic? It is! It takes time and consistency and a great system. And **you** can do it. My goal with this book and my other services for real estate agents is to help you achieve this. Now get started!

## Key Takeaways:

1. _____

2. _____

3. _____

4. _____

5. _____

## Chapter Seven

# Lever #5: Affiliations

---

A lever most people forget about is affiliations. When you are affiliated with someone or something, you get the network, credentials, reputation and benefits from that affiliation. This can be a huge lever for you as a real estate salesperson. Let's explore what types of affiliations would be good levers in your real estate sales business.

**Company**
Most agents start with affiliating with a brokerage after getting their license. This is a natural and great start to your career. As you continue into your career, you may find it advantageous to switch the brokerage you are affiliated with. The most common reasons people leave a brokerage for another is lack of support. The support can mean training, coaching, teaching or a friendly atmosphere.

My recommendations for finding a great brokerage to align with is simple. First, identify what your big vision is and outline some simple steps to accomplish that goal. Second, look for a company that offers plenty of free classes, taught at the office, that you can go to each month. Third, look for a supportive office manager or broker who can commit to your success. Share your goals and make sure they can support you in that journey.

Example: if you want to start a sales team and sell 100 homes per year, find out first if that manager/ broker has successfully guided another agent in the office to accomplish that goal. If you find out that they have not, you want to keep looking for someone who has.

Next, look for an office environment where agents are doing the teaching, mentoring and guiding of other agents. You want to be part of an office that has an abundance mindset, not a scarcity mindset. In practical terms, agents are willing and happy to show you tips, secrets and strategies to help you succeed. If the office environment is overly competitive and agents withhold ideas and aggressively try to top each other, you may not get peer advice, which would be very helpful for you.

Last but not least, I would find an office with a very strong reputation in the market you are going to sell in. If the office is well known and liked, you are more likely to get a positive response to your prospecting and marketing.

On another level, you can choose a brokerage that has a large national or international reach. There are a few main benefits from this. First, you get big brand power that most clients like to see. Second, you get the tools and systems from that big company to use in your local business. Third, you can network with other agents around the world and get real estate referrals more readily. Last, you can participate in national events and seminars that only affiliates can join.

## Team or Agent Partner

Once you have affiliated with a great brokerage, you can also consider joining another agent's team (if you haven't already started your own team). If you are eventually looking to build your own team, it may not be a bad idea to start with a successful team to learn how an effective team's systems work. Being an individual agent is much different than running a team. You may decide that you like working with another agent's team or you may decide that you want to start your own team. Alternatively, you may decide that you don't want to have anything to do with a team and stay working as an individual agent. There isn't a right answer. You must decide this for yourself.

## Trade Associations

The National Association of Realtors® has a ton of resources to help agents. They have a magazine, their website, special discounts, trainings, national events, support to state and local associations, and more. Most licensed real estate agents and brokers are members of the National Association of Realtors® already. I wanted to make sure that we have that box checked. Being an official Realtor® has benefits.

Don't forget that you also should belong to your state's association and a local association. There are benefits (and requirements that you must meet) when you join your local Multiple Listing Service. I also highly recommend getting involved with the volunteer leadership side of these organizations.

Early in my career, I started volunteering at my local Board of Realtors®. That turned into teaching classes at the board. Then I was asked to sit on a committee for technology. Then they asked me to be the chair of that committee. Next, I was asked to be on the board of directors. After participating in that for a couple of years I was asked to be the President-Elect and eventually the President. I then served as the immediate past President and then back to a board member. I have also been the emcee at about a dozen events for the association.

Through all those volunteer positions, I have met hundreds of agents and expanded my circle of influence. Throughout the 16 years, I have had many instances where my connections with agents I met while serving have helped me help my real estate clients. Knowing the other agent before you enter into a transaction is very valuable. That is leverage that you might not be thinking about, but you should!

**Chamber/Networking Groups**
Being involved with local chambers and networking groups has been a great experience. Similar to the story above, I have had many roles within my local chamber, everything from committee participation to committee chair, to board of directors, to emcee, to the President position. Not only have I met some great friends over the years, I have also earned the right to sell homes for the people I met. I can say that over time, these warm networking relationships have led to over $100,000 worth

of commissions earned. I have also learned about things happening in our community sooner and in more detail than the average person would find out about. And, I had the opportunity to meet city leaders and managers to help my clients achieve their goals. More leverage!

**Online Groups**
For those of you who don't know, Facebook is the biggest media outlet on the planet. And it is also a great way to build relationships with people you would never otherwise have met. If you type in some kind of interest or hobby, you can find a group for it. For example, there is a Facebook group called Lab Coat Agents with over 100,000 real estate agents networking and sharing content.

Last year, I joined an online business group called 100X Acceleration. I met Christian entrepreneurs from all over the world online in a private Facebook group. Then I liked the group so much that I decided to go to an in-person event they were having on the other side of the country. I spent four days with these people from all over the world and fostered even deeper relationships. The knowledge, understanding and wisdom I have gained is more than I could have asked for or imagined. It all started from an online group. Writing my first book, *The Lord's Prayer for Entrepreneurs,* and this second one here are tangible results of my involvement with this group so far. The individuals in the group have given me the encouragement and push I needed to achieve my goals. Don't forget about or underestimate online groups as an amazing form of leverage.

## Key Takeaways:

1. _____

2. _____

3. _____

4. _____

5. _____

# Chapter Eight

## Lever# 6 Database

---

Many Realtors® know that the highest return on their investment dollar is in your database. Why is this? Zig Ziglar says, "Help enough people get what they want and you will get what you want." Well, if you continue to help people and provide massive value to them, they turn into happy clients. The likelihood is that they will do more business with you or refer you to someone they know who will also buy or sell a property. A happy client is the best way to build a business.

A majority of real estate buyers and sellers, when surveyed after the real estate transaction, say they would use their real estate agent again in the future. But only less than 20% actually do. Why is this? In my estimation, there are several reasons. I believe the top reason due to most agents doing a poor job of staying in touch with clients after the sale. It's the old "love 'em and leave 'em strategy." This is not a great way to build a sustainable business. Since we are focusing on leverage in this book, the best lever you have for acquiring new clients is your database.

The size of your business or income is equal to the size of the database you have acquired. To clarify, the database includes previous clients or other people you have met.

Some agents break their database down further into two categories: "met" and "unmet" lists. Here is the difference. If you have had a direct conversation with a person, then you have met them. If you have an online lead, a postcard address or some other form of contact, that is usually considered "unmet."

Many of my real estate sales over the years have come from my database, specifically, the people who I have met. These are either networking contacts, friends, family, acquaintances, or past clients. When it comes to working your database, there are a few important steps involved. I suppose this topic could be an entire book in itself, so we will keep it short and sweet here. On average, people buy five homes in their life: a starter home, first move up, second move up, a luxury or investment property, and a retirement home. How many do you want to be involved with?

First, find a database software program you can use, and start using it. As we discussed in the Systems and Tools chapter, the best Customer Relationship Manager (CRM) software is the one you *actually* use. Next, determine a plan on how you will stay in touch with those in your database. Plan out your year's calendar in advance and schedule your "touches" (contact points). Make your touch program automatic and specific. For example, we at The Tye Group have a schedule of 40 touches per year. This includes things like our monthly newsletters, an email invite to our four (quarterly) client-only events, phone calls before the events to remind clients they are invited, a magazine subscription they receive in the mail each month, and holiday cards. Sending these reminders and touches to our database is part of the job description of our team's Director of Operations. Because we never lose touch with them, this is one of the reasons our clients say they love to refer their friends and family to us.

All new team members who come on board with us must contribute at least 100 people (they have met) to the database. This helps us grow as a team, but we always give those back to an agent if they leave the team.

**Oh, hello?**
What do you say when you call a client to try and "stay in touch?" Never, ever call a client to just "check in." We all value our time and don't want it wasted. Instead, you should always add value.

"Hi, I have some information for you!"
"I've been noticing this trend; I see this happening in the market."
"We have this great event we want to invite you to."
"Did you get the magazine we sent you?"

You may also want to categorize database people into groups. Categorize them into A, B, or C clients. The "A" category are your best, most loyal, VIPs. They have bought or sold from you in the past or have referred you to someone who has. The "B" category are past clients who you had positive experiences with, warm leads you are nurturing and people you have met in person who you feel you have potential to eventually do business with. The "C" category is everyone else in your database.

Regarding events, they are fun ways to engage your database. Have an event coordinator on staff or have systems in place so that everyone on the team has a role for each event. Have a defined process for before the event, during and for follow up after. Here are some ideas for client events you can reach out to your database with:

- Holiday pie giveaways
- Movie night
- Santa photos
- Father-daughter dance
- Baseball game
- Easter egg hunt
- "Dog Days of Summer" event
- Petting zoo day
- Pick up spring flowers at the office day

Your clients and people in your database always want value. What would they find valuable from you? Consider putting together a list of preferred vendors. Put your favorite lender, title company, roofer, painter, plumber, electrician, handyman, contractor, basement water proofer, etc., on the list and your clients will really appreciate that. Be the "Angie's List" to your database. When they think about real estate, you want them to think about you first and the many connections you have.

You can also partner with restaurant or entertainment providers in your area with coupons, buy one, get one free (BOGO) discounts, offers, promotions, free chances, etc. This is a way for you to connect to new business owners and managers of establishments in your area too. This is a great way to build your database and add value to both sides.

A great benefit you can add to your past buyers is to provide them with an annual CMA (Comparative Market Analysis) report to them so they can see how their home value is doing. This is really cool and a nice end-of-year activity when the market is typically slower.

Don't forget to have someone on the team sending out handwritten notes daily. If you can send out 3-5 notes every workday, imagine the impact you will have on your past clients. This goes a long way and costs very little. Keep track of birthdays, send a note if you hear they've had a difficult season, be an uplifting voice in their day, show you care.

When you get to the point in your career where you start understanding investment properties, you can help people build wealth for a great way to save for retirement or college. When you help people create wealth and security, they will refer you real estate business too. We have an investment seminar every other month at our office. We invite our whole database. This has led to our past clients becoming real estate investors and very loyal fans.

**Begin with the end in mind.**
As you start adding people to your database, make sure you are collecting critical information. Build something that will be useful and easy to work with later! There is an old saying: "garbage in, garbage out." If you don't collect key information for your database, then it will diminish the value you get back out of it. I highly recommend collecting at least these seven categories:

**Seven Database Input Areas:**
1. Name of primary client contact and spouse
2. Email addresses of primary and spouse
3. Phone numbers for primary and spouse
4. Current home address (make sure to update)
5. Source of this lead (client referral, open house, Facebook ad, etc.)
6. Status of client (past client, buyer, seller, nurture)
7. Notes about them (you may forget critical info if you don't)

**Agent Referrals**
Many successful agents have used leverage by building huge referral networks with other real estate agents across the country. They send clients to other agents; clients who they cannot serve geographically or due to the type of real estate transaction. For example, I have sent my clients to agents I trust in California, Texas, Florida and other places.

I have also referred some complex commercial deals to agents here in Cincinnati when I didn't feel we were the most qualified to handle them. These referral agents should also go into your database, and you should nurture those relationships just as you would your own clients (especially if that agent has sent you a real buyer or seller). This goes the other way as well. As you refer another agent a real estate client, you should put that agent in your database too. Keep these relationships warm, and over time you may be surprised on the number of repeat sales you will gain from agent-to-agent referrals. Most referral-sending agents will ask for a 25% referral fee off of the gross commission earned on the sale (or sales) related to that referral. This fee can be negotiated. If you work for a smaller brokerage that does not have a national or international network, I would recommend joining some Facebook referral groups to expand your reach to as many agents as possible. Please make sure to foster real relationships and only send referrals to agents you have vetted for your client.

Now, here comes the shameless plug. If you need a great agent to send your Greater Cincinnati, Ohio, real estate referrals to, please send them to me and my team. We do honor a 25% referral fee for you and will take great care of your client. Now, send referrals to **derek@derektye.com**. Okay, the shameless plug is over. You can resume the book now. :)

Once you have people in your database and you are

touching them regularly with great value adds, you are on your way to building a big business. Don't forget to make your database a powerful leverage tool in your real estate bag. This is truly the most sustainable way to long term success in the real estate business. Now on to some fun ways to continue your success!

## Key Takeaways:

1. _____

2. _____

3. _____

4. _____

5. _____

*Chapter Nine*

*Lever #7: Content Creation*

---

What if you could have new, potential clients contacting you from content you have already created? What if that content came from some area of interest you really like talking about? This is one way to create leverage that many real estate agents never think about. This is more of an advanced, creative area of real estate leverage, but very important. Here are some great ways to create "evergreen" content; content that is always working for you.

**Blog**
Millions of blogs, so little time, right? Well, very specific topics on blogs still see thousands of readers every year. So what could you blog about? If you are into golfing in your community, you could write about each of your local golf courses (and of course the homes and neighborhoods that surround each course). You could write about your favorite hobby and tie it into real estate somehow. I used to blog about properties that I listed and tell a little story about that home, along with pictures. That content is still around in Google for all to see. Some of those blogs are 14 years old but still get clicks because of certain key words people are searching for. If you want to be an expert in your town, start blogging about something that interests you.

You could even start a blog on dining or shopping in your area. People buy from those who they know, trust and feel comfortable with. This is a great way to gain trust.

**Facebook Groups**

There are thousands of examples of people who've started Facebook groups. Finding a niche that you really like to work with and focusing on that one thing is really important. I know a guy who started a Facebook group for Christian Entrepreneurs (people who are like him). He started finding more and more people who liked his style and belief system. After about 18 months, he now has thousands of people in the group and a massive email list. He has started charging for events, coaching and teaching and is still growing every week. For local real estate, this could be a mom's group, a neighborhood group, an alumni group from your school or any other focused collection of people. Make the content interesting and centered around a targeted theme and the group will grow.

**Podcast**

Podcasting is a great way to spread a message with your local expertise. I have seen firsthand how the power of this media can help build a business. My wife started a podcast a few years ago. She wanted to talk about her journey of health and specifically wanted to explore the Ketogenic Diet. As she listened to other podcasts on the subject, they seemed to be all about the diet. She wanted to showcase the lifestyle and sustainability aspect of keto as a way of living. So she learned how to record a show on her computer and started publishing episodes. A couple years later, she had crossed the 400,000 downloads mark! People have found her all over the world and love the content she puts out. One of the great things about a podcast is that the content stays out there for a really long time. If they have a specific topic or question they need help with, she can point them back to a certain episode and they can listen to that.

Podcasting also creates other opportunities. There are events, seminars and speaking engagements Jessica has been invited to after people have heard her on her podcast. She also has been invited to be a guest on many other podcasts.

Podcasting also creates trust. After someone has listened to several episodes, they begin to trust her more and more. As a real estate agent, imagine walking into a listing appointment and the person has already heard you talk about the local market for several hours. This is the ultimate trust builder.

**YouTube**
Could you have your own YouTube channel? Many real estate agents use YouTube to build a strong audience. Similar to podcasting, you don't have to have millions of subscribers to make this work for you. Years ago, I hired a videographer to go around Loveland, Ohio, and take some video footage. Before he went out, I wrote up a blog post about the town. The videographer used my blog post to know where to go and what videos to take. After he

recorded footage, he then narrated the video and made some edits. We put that video on our Tye Group YouTube channel, and it has been on there for ten years!

The Loveland video has been watched thousands of times and is especially helpful for people who are new to the area. It's like a video commercial on how wonderful it is to live there. I originally spent $1,000 on the video, and I would say it has helped me gain trust and show buyers and sellers that I am an authority in the Loveland, Ohio, market.

This is something you can do for free now with all the latest editing software built into most smart phones. My recommendation is to find a part of your town that you feel comfortable talking about. Write up a nice, 3 to 5-minute description of why you like the town. Go around and film some video of those highlights, then publish it to YouTube. Don't forget to use key words and enter tags into the upload tool. After your first video, then go out and make another one!

If you are working with a new buyer or someone from out of town, make sure to send them the link to your video. This will add credibility and make you stand out from anyone else they are considering working with. Video is huge leverage to establish confidence. People hire people. One of the best ways to make yourself human is to be on video. So make sure that part of that video includes you!

## Book

Writing a book may sound like a daunting task. After writing my last book, the second one came much easier! But you don't have to write a huge novel to get a benefit out of it. I heard of one agent who wrote a book on "how to buy a home" in his hometown. He published it on Amazon and it is more of a guide about local areas, neighborhoods, etc. Think about this genius idea: when he meets a new buyer, he gives them a copy of his book. It would be cool to buy a home from the author, right?

I hope this inspires you to think outside the box a little. A book can be an e-book product too. If you type out a guide on your favorite software and save it as a PDF, you can then easily email the e-book to potential clients. Add images you've taken around town.

Also, think about this: use your book as a lead magnet on your website to get email addresses from potential clients. Offer your book free in exchange for a lead's contact info. You can find great writing coaches out there to get you started or just ask a friend to help. Either way, writing a book is a great way to add credibility and make you the local market expert.

## Key Takeaways:

1. _____

2. _____

3. _____

4. _____

5. _____

# *Summary*

If you are like me, you want to do all of these levers tomorrow! Maybe you have an ambitious spirit, too, and want to tackle them all...all at the same time. My recommendation is to master one at a time. I wrote this book in a certain order, offering levers in a practical path for someone just starting this business. Feel free to work on whichever lever is the most appropriate for you right now, wherever you are in your real estate sales journey.

The most common question I get after doing this business for 16 years is "what would you do if you had to start over again? Well, here is what I would do today:

First, I would align myself with key people. This would be a broker/manager, then a real estate mentor or coach. I would find people in my real estate office to bounce ideas off of. Then, I would get an accountability partner.

Next, I would work on some tech and online pieces. I'd get a good email address and become really familiar with a good email software. Then I would thoroughly learn about my local MLS system and its tools. Building myself a website that allowed potential clients to search for ALL local MLS listings and register as a user would be next. You ultimately need to build a database and keep potential clients in your care. If you send them to another company's website to search listings, you have a strong risk of losing them to a competing agent.

Next, I would learn to master my time – my morning routine and my time spent at the office. I would read the book *The One Thing* a few times and really dig into the concept of asking the focusing question.

When it comes to sales, I would do everything I could to get listings. I would work open houses for other agents, door knock in neighborhoods I liked and call around in those neighborhoods looking for sellers.

I would join a local Board of Realtors® and go to as many free classes as possible. I would join a committee and learn as much as I could about how the Board of Realtors® worked. I would network with those other agents and get to know them.

I would get my database up and running. Is your broker already using database software? If so, I recommend using that. It will probably be free for you and you will have free training and support around it. My goal would be to add at least one person to my database every workday. I would put a plan together on what to do with the people in my database and stay in touch with them at least 40 times per year.

When I had done all of these things, I would probably write up a guidebook on buying a home in my town. I would

# Summary

include a list of all the neighborhoods and describe the supporting community around them. I would convert it to a PDF guide and email it to as many people as I thought would use it. I would set it up as a lead magnet on my website too, so I could start getting email addresses and add those potential clients to my database.

I like to win. I like to make money and I love to serve people. You probably do too. That is okay! Keep in mind that entrepreneurs have a strong desire to *win*! We are *not* good losers. We never get used to losing. We also like to be on winning teams and pick other winners to come along with us on our journeys. If you look around to your left and right, who are you surrounding yourself with?

For now, I will leave you with this. Do the best you can every day. Even making a 1% improvement every day in your habits, your time management, your prospecting, and life will lead to huge results eventually. Just keep improving and growing every day, and you will win at life!

> If you want to continue learning more real estate success skills, check out our group coaching program and training materials at **www.KingdomRealEstateAgents.com** or join us on Facebook in the "Seller Listings Mastery Group."

## Key Takeaways:

1. _____

2. _____

3. _____

4. _____

5. _____

# *Resources and Routines:*

**My ideal daily routine Monday to Friday:**
- I fast through breakfast completely, or mix a high-fat, no-carb coffee in my blender (like a latte)
- Use the infrared sauna for 30 minutes, while reading or listening to my Bible-in-a-year plan
- Prayer
- Affirmations
- Read out loud my goals
- Journal events of the past 24 hours
- Journal gratitude
- Thirty minutes of email
- Two hours of lead generation and lead follow-up
- Return calls from morning
- Healthy Lunch (in my opinion that would be high fat, low carb, moderate protein)
- Social media posts and content creation
- Go on appointments I set earlier
- Negotiate any deals I have going
- Healthy dinner with the family by 6:00 p.m.
- Spend time with my wife and kids (outside on my land if possible)
- Read 15 minutes before bed, usually by 10:30 p.m.

**I recommend keeping your mind renewed daily, and always be learning something new!**
- Time block for daily reading time
- Listen to great podcasts
- Listen to great audio books
- Read printed books
- Attend a regular small group study or book club

**I recommend time blocking these things:**
- Quarterly and annual vacation (spouse only trip and family trip)
- Daily tasks
- Weekly tasks
- Quarterly business planning
- Personal health (chiropractor, dentist, acupuncture, massage, nutritionist, yoga, etc.)
- Fun activities
- Serving others

**Here are some systems I employ in my businesses:**
- CRM (customer relationship manager). Currently I use a spreadsheet and Follow Up Boss
- Client events to treat them to some fun (at least four per year)
- Phone dialers for outbound calling efficiency
- Coaching for myself
- Scripts for me and all my employees

Choose your library carefully. What you read will help determine your future. Here are some books I have read (business and real estate) and would highly recommend:
- *Every Good Endeavor,* Timothy Keller
- *Business Secrets from the Bible,* Daniel Lapin
- *The One Thing,* Gary Keller
- *Pitch Anything,* Oren Klaff
- *Never Split the Difference,* Chris Voss
- *Start with Why,* Simon Sinek
- *Pitch Anything,* Oren Klaff
- *Never Split the Difference,* Chris Voss
- *Start with Why,* Simon Sinek
- *The Ultimate Jim Rohn Library,* Jim Rohn
- *The 4-Hour Workweek,* Timothy Ferriss
- *The Alchemist,* Paulo Coelho
- *Titan: The Life of John D Rockefeller,* Ron Chernow
- *Millionaire Real Estate Agent,* Garry Keller
- *Seven Levels of Communication,* Michael Maher
- *Think and Grow Rich,* Napolean Hill
- *How to Win Friends and Influence People,* Dale Carnegie
- *Seven Habits of Highly Effective People,* Stephen Covey
- *Shift,* Gary Keller
- *The Millionaire Real Estate Investor,* Gary Keller

**Podcasts I listen to:**
- 100X with Pedro Adao
- Linda McKissack Everything Life and Business
- Church for Entrepreneurs
- Kingdom Driven Entrepreneur
- Elevation Church

- Keto Lifestyle with Jessica Tye
- Craig Groeschel leadership Podcast

**Affirmations I say out loud at the beginning of each workday:**
- We care about our clients more than selling.
- We impact our clients' lives positively every day.
- I am happy, healthy and it's going to be a great day!
- We provide the best possible service available to our clients.
- People love to work with us!
- We love drumming up new business and we take advantage of all possible networking opportunities.
- I am a money magnet!
- I do not take rejection personally.
- I am confident when asking for business and referrals.
- I provide value to my clients and those I wish to add to my fan club.
- I speak positively about my business.
- I will reach my goals only with God's blessing.
- I always choose to do the right thing.
- I am a great husband, a great father, a great leader and a great friend!
- The future is bright!
- I am becoming wealthier every day.
- I am learning to master my time.
- I choose faith over fear.

**My mission statement I read aloud each work morning:**
- My personal mission is to build, inspire and love people so they live up to their God-given calling and live life to the fullest.

*Now, write one for yourself!*

# *Testimonials*

"It has been an absolute honor to work with you the past few years. You are a kind man with much integrity...and so knowledgeable about real estate! Here is to many more years of friendship! Blessings, with love and respect."
— *Dede and Anthony Muñoz*

"Derek is a truly altruistic and authentic man – giving in every aspect, an invaluable professional resource and wonderful person to know. As I was coming into the real estate world from another industry, knowledge, guidance and leadership were critical components for me to find. Derek, as one of our investors and top agents, provided this for me...and so much more! Whether you are looking for a partner on your God journey, looking for a coaching program or a podcast or a book to help you, you can count on Derek to serve you at a high level, deliver value and do it with a smile and caring heart. Enjoy the journey!"
— *Jeff House, Keller Williams*

"I believe we meet certain people at times when we need them to open a door for our next path. After a few conversations over a listing Derek was selling, I quickly knew he was a person I was connected to for a reason. Instantly relating to Derek's personal and professional values, I knew he was somebody I would like to work with on a consistent basis. Eighteen months later, my own

business is thriving with the assistance of his coaching and mentorship. I'm grateful for that first 15-minute random phone call, as I'm now designing and living the life I want as a result of the relationship I've developed with him."
— Luke Luther, Keller Williams Realty

"I am going into my 25th year in the real estate industry and have had the privilege to work with Derek Tye for the last two of those years. As the broker for my office, I see my fair share of agent-related issues with transactions. Not the case with Derek. His work and life are guided by his high standards, ethics and Christian background. He is an absolute pleasure to work with and an example for new and existing agents on how to run a business and live life to the fullest. Derek was instrumental in my decision to join Keller Williams Seven Hills. He took the time to meet with me personally, one-on-one, during my transition to answer some of my questions and assure me that he would be there to help me in any way possible. He makes the office a better place to work with his professionalism, his ethics and high levels of expectations."
— Chris Parchman, Principal Broker, KW7H

"Derek is an inspiration to the office. He has not only inspired me to be the best that I can be, he also brings this inspiration and encouragement to each and every person he meets. Derek possesses an incredible knowledge of business and has even helped in the growth of my spirituality and health. No matter how big or small the problem may be, he is always there to lend a helping hand,

never asking for anything in return."
— *Rebecca Geiger, The Geiger Team*

"Derek is an exceptional leader in the real estate field. He holds himself and those around him to the highest of standards, and that is evident in all aspects of his professional and personal life. He has a servant's heart for people and is unashamedly willing to help anyone who asks. I recently came to Derek to discuss how faith can positively intersect with my real estate career, and he graciously gave his time and knowledge to me. I walked away from the conversation feeling much better about seeking extraordinary success so I could carry on what God has put in my heart for helping the less fortunate. I know I will come to Derek in the future for additional guidance. He is selfless in his approach to people. The other person's success is what Derek hopes to help them achieve."
— *Jennifer McGillis, Realtor®*

"Derek and I have gotten into several short, impactful conversations about my business. It has always started out as a small question that he turns into a coaching session, and I always feel like *man, I should've recorded that*! The nuggets of wisdom he hands out so charitably have been crucial in shaping my business this year. I can't thank Derek enough for all of his help with my business and life."
— *Flor de Maria McNally, De Maria Team*

"I worked with Derek as an admin in his real estate business for six years. During the multi-step interview process, the idea Derek wanted to make sure I understood was: "We do the right thing, the right way, and the money will come." Derek challenged his entire team to work with an abundance mentality and to do the right thing for our clients and other agents, no matter what it costs. I watched Derek lose money several times, by doing the right thing, but my respect for him only grew, as did that of our team members. Working behind the scenes, I saw the numbers go up and down, I saw the deals fall apart, I saw the personal and professional tragedies. I learned so much working with Derek. In fact, I remember asking him once to teach me how to dream, how to set goals and accomplish them. I have to say he is the most consistent person I have ever met. Not perfect by any stretch. He has ups and downs like anyone, but because he believes so strongly in his God, himself and his principles, he always comes back to center."

— *Claudia Hrinda, former Team Administrator*

"You are always open to helping a new agent, with a world of experience and knowledge, but most important is your heart and your sweet family. You have managed to keep centered on the humanity of what we do as real estate agents, and I am most sure that our Lord is well pleased." — *Rose Manibusan, KW*

"It has been my privilege to work for Derek Tye. I could quote the many accomplishments and accolades he has received, but the side that I like to bear witness to is his personal side. He takes great joy in each member's

accomplishments. Derek challenges and mentors his team in order for them to stretch and attain higher goals by setting a big vision. Derek always makes time for his team and others. He gives 100% of himself no matter what the mission involves. Derek is a natural-born leader and teacher. He knows what talents God has given him. He is obedient to our Father and knows what he is called to do and not to do. Derek loves being a REALTOR®. He is honest and forthcoming with his clients, even when the truth might be difficult for the client to hear. Derek cares for his clients and treats them as if they are part of his family, because in his mind, they are. Derek consistently delivers excellence and is a humble man who continues to grow in understanding by always reaching out to new mentors and praying for God's will in his life. Without a doubt, those who have reason to come in contact with Derek are always blessed."
— *Lisa Cook, Greyline Technologies*

"Derek shows up 100% every day in every way, I could not ask for a better overall person to be in business with!"
— *Chrissy Ward, Chrissy Ward Team*

# *About Derek Tye*

"My personal mission is to build, inspire and love people to live up to their God-given calling and live life to the fullest." —Derek Tye

Derek Tye, is an award-winning REALTOR® in the Cincinnati, Ohio, area. Starting in the real estate business in 2004, Derek and his wife, Jessica, built a successful real estate team that continues to this day. Derek and Jessica are also real estate investors and have enjoyed building a portfolio of short-term rental homes near their home in Loveland, Ohio. Derek's love of teaching others to reach their fullest potential has recently prompted him to write two books. His first book, written in 2019, is *The Lord's Prayer for Entrepreneurs: Unlock Success and Build God's Kingdom Through Your Business*. His second book, *Seven Levers for Success in Selling Real Estate*, was published in 2020. Both are available on Amazon in print and digital versions.

Derek and his wife, Jessica, have five children and enjoy traveling and playing around on their hobby farm in Loveland, Ohio. Derek also enjoys mountain biking, kayaking, hiking and playing frisbee.

## Credentials:

Top 1% U.S. Real Estate Agent in 2019 by sold volume
Past President and Director of the Southern Ohio Association of REALTORS®
1,400 Properties Sold for over $300,000,000
2018 Top Sales Team/Group, Southern Ohio Association of REALTORS®
2018 Top Social Media Team in Cincinnati: ThreeBestRated.com
Investor in a Keller Williams Realty Franchise
Owner in multiple investment properties
Realtor of the Year: Southern Ohio Association of REALTORS® 2010
Team Average of 5/5 Star User Rankings with over 100 reviews on Zillow, Realtor.com®, Yelp and Google
Realtor® since 2004
Author
Speaker

If you need a great agent to send your Greater Cincinnati, Ohio, real estate referrals to, please send them to me and my team. We do honor a 25% referral fee for you, and we will take great care of your client.

Reach out today at derek@derektye.com
www.DerekTye.com
www.KingdomRealEstateAgents.com

# *Speaking*

Looking for a dynamic, knowledgeable speaker for your organization's next event? Contact us now for more information on having Derek speak for your group, leadership team, training event, conference, webinar, or podcast.

Derek can tailor speaking topics for your group or event on themes such as:

- Leverage in Real Estate
- Team Building
- Mindset

To book Derek, contact him at derek@derektye.com.

www.ingramcontent.com/pod-product-compliance
Lightning Source LLC
Chambersburg PA
CBHW071417210526
45465CB00001B/431